Original title:
The Solstice Silence

Copyright © 2024 Swan Charm
All rights reserved.

Author: Sabrina Sarvik
ISBN HARDBACK: 978-9908-1-1420-0
ISBN PAPERBACK: 978-9908-1-1421-7
ISBN EBOOK: 978-9908-1-1422-4

Ghosts of Sunlight Past

Golden beams dance on the ground,
Whispers of warmth, a joyful sound.
Laughter echoes, shadows play,
Memories bright, from yesterday.

Children chase fireflies in the night,
Every flicker, pure delight.
The sky adorned with twinkling stars,
While we share stories, near and far.

Night's Gentle Caress

Beneath the moon's soft silver glow,
The world is hushed, a magic flow.
Crickets serenade the evening air,
With each note, dreams whisper and share.

Candles flicker, a tranquil light,
Wrapping us in warmth tonight.
Softly swaying, the trees embrace,
As time slows down, we find our place.

Reflections in the Icy Pond

Mirrored stillness, a winter's dance,
Frozen beauty, a fleeting glance.
The world in white, pure in its grace,
Nature's art, a tranquil space.

Children bundled, laughter bright,
Ice-skating under soft starlight.
In every swirl, joy intertwines,
Moments captured, like delicate signs.

Serenity Wrapped in Shadows

Embers glow in the twilight's embrace,
Soft shadows gather, finding their place.
The hush of night blankets the ground,
In this serene depth, peace is found.

Songs of the heart weave through the air,
Melodies soft, a tender share.
Whispers of wishes in the dark,
Fueling dreams with a gentle spark.

Veil of Winter's Embrace

Snowflakes dance in the moonlight glow,
Children's laughter, a warm tableau.
Firelight flickers, a cozy retreat,
Joyful hearts with every heartbeat.

Carols echo through the crisp, clean air,
Festive cheer, a world stripped bare.
Wreathed in pine, a scent divine,
Season of love, when all align.

Celestial Pause

Stars twinkle bright in a velvet sea,
Moments shared, just you and me.
Candles flicker, shadows play,
Night's embrace makes worries stray.

The world feels light under the moon's kiss,
Every glance, a moment of bliss.
Laughter bubbles, joy takes flight,
Whispers of magic fill the night.

Emptiness of the Twilight Hour

Shadows stretch as the sun dips low,
Hope and dreams in the twilight flow.
A golden hush wraps the sleepy town,
Moments linger, no hints of frown.

Colors blend in a palette of peace,
Time slows down, worries cease.
A breath held in the gentle air,
Quietude reigns, a moment rare.

Hushed Moments of Reflection

Sipping warmth by the fireside,
Memories play like a gentle tide.
Comfort found in the still of night,
Soul's embrace in softest light.

Each gentle whisper, each fleeting thought,
Bring to heart what love has taught.
In these moments, we find our way,
Guided by hope, come what may.

Surrender to the Hush

The evening glows with twinkling light,
As laughter dances, dreams take flight.
Soft music sways, a gentle thrill,
In the calm embrace, hearts softly still.

Moments linger, sweet and bright,
Under stars that shimmer in the night.
With every cheer, the world feels warm,
A tapestry of joy, our spirits transform.

Echoes of joy flicker like flames,
Fleeting whispers, unclaimed names.
In this hush, we freely roam,
Finding together, a rhythm, a home.

As time drifts on with tender grace,
We lose ourselves in this cherished space.
Every heartbeat, a festive song,
In surrendering now, we all belong.

Reverie in a Frozen World

Snowflakes dance in the silver light,
Crystal whispers, a blanket tight.
Frozen moments, capturing dreams,
In shimmering silence, magic beams.

Candles flicker, a warm embrace,
Around the fire, we find our place.
Laughter threads through the frosty air,
In this wonderland, joys we share.

Every breath a puff of white,
In this reverie, hearts ignite.
Together we weave a tapestry bright,
In a frozen world, our spirits unite.

With every sparkle, we feel alive,
In the hush of winter, our dreams thrive.
Beneath the stars, this night so sweet,
In a frozen world, our souls meet.

The Language of Quiet Nights

Moonlight spills through the gentle trees,
Whispers linger, floating like breeze.
In the stillness, secrets unfold,
The language of quiet is softly told.

Voices muted, yet spirits soar,
In the silence, we seek for more.
Every glance, a story shared,
In these moments, deeply paired.

Crickets hum a soothing tune,
Beneath the watchful eye of the moon.
And as the night wraps us in peace,
Our hearts find solace, a sweet release.

Hidden wonders in the quiet folds,
Glimmers of joy that nature holds.
In the stillness, we truly see,
The language of night speaks to you and me.

Anthems of the Silent Sky

Stars align in a cosmic dance,
Filling the night with a silent trance.
Each twinkle a note in a grand refrain,
Anthems woven, joyous and plain.

The sky whispers tales of old,
In every shimmer, legends unfold.
With arms wide open, we gaze high,
Underneath the vast, endless sky.

Hearts beat softly in this embrace,
Finding rhythm in the universe's grace.
In the softness of night, we can sigh,
Together, forever, under this sky.

So let us gather with dreams to ignite,
Beneath the stars, our spirits take flight.
With every heartbeat, we sing along,
In the silence, we find our song.

Nature's Breathless Interlude

Beneath the trees, the laughter rings,
Children dance, their joy takes flight,
Sunlight glimmers on the stream,
Nature blooms in pure delight.

Petals swirl in fragrant air,
Colors burst in warm embrace,
Whispers soft, the breezes share,
Time slows down in this sweet space.

Breezes kiss the orchard's face,
Joyful songs fill every heart,
In this moment's gentle grace,
Life and love shall never part.

As twilight comes, the stars ignite,
A tapestry of dreams unfold,
Together 'neath the painted night,
Our spirits dance, and tales are told.

The Gathering of Winter's Veil

Snowflakes twirl like festive lights,
Blanketing the world in white,
Fires crackle, warmth invites,
Gathering close on winter nights.

Laughter echoes through the air,
Mugs held high, spirits combine,
Friends and family everywhere,
Together toast with hearts divine.

Candles flicker, shadows play,
Stories shared, love intertwines,
In this hush of winter's sway,
Magic glows with bright designs.

As dawn brings forth the softest hue,
Hope awakens with each ray,
In winter's arms, we feel anew,
Celebrating life today.

Echoes of Firelight

Around the glow, we gather near,
Crackling flames and joyful cheer,
As stories weave through night's embrace,
Firelight dances on each face.

Drumming hearts and spirits raise,
In twilight's warm, embracing glow,
Each flicker sparks a memory's blaze,
Laughter mingles with the flow.

Beneath the night, the stars enthrall,
We share our dreams, both big and small,
This gathering, a magic band,
Together here, we brightly stand.

With every spark, our hopes ignite,
In this moment, pure delight,
Voices join, a harmony,
Echoes of firelight, we're free.

Dreaming in the Chill

Whispers in the frosty air,
Snowflakes dance, a cosmic flight,
Underneath the moon's soft glare,
Dreamers gather, hearts alight.

Sipping cocoa, fireside glow,
Laughter twinkles like the stars,
In this dreamland, time moves slow,
We share our hopes, erase the scars.

Blankets wrapped in colors bright,
Stories woven through the night,
Each breath a puff of gleaming white,
Embraced by love, our spirits take flight.

As whispers fade into the dawn,
Memories linger, sweet and still,
In every heart, a warmth is drawn,
We wake anew, yet dream in chill.

Shadows of Solitude

In the glow of lantern light,
Laughter dances in the night.
Joyful hearts and spirits free,
Merriment for all to see.

Festive songs fill up the air,
Everyone has smiles to share.
Under stars, our worries fade,
In this bliss, we all cascade.

Colors twinkle, bright and bold,
Stories, secrets, all retold.
With each cheer, the shadows fade,
In this night, we are remade.

Let the music play and sway,
As shadows dance, we'll boldly stay.
In radiant warmth, let's reside,
Together under joy's sweet tide.

When Darkness Holds Court

Gather close, the night is near,
Moonlight shimmers, bright and clear.
In the stillness, laughter grows,
As the festive spirit flows.

Candles flicker, soft and warm,
Crickets chirp, their midnight charm.
In the hush, a chorus sings,
Joyful hope as daylight swings.

With every toast, the dark retreats,
Glorious moments, time repeats.
Underneath the starlit dome,
Each heart finds its welcome home.

Together we defy the night,
Woven whispers of delight.
In this realm where dreams ignite,
We stand as one in purest light.

Silence Wraps the Twilight

As the day begins to close,
Glistening dew on petals rose.
Colors merge, a canvas bright,
In the hush of coming night.

Twinkling lights begin to gleam,
Echoes of a gentle dream.
Friendship bonds, a circle wide,
In this moment, hearts collide.

Softly laughter fills the air,
Cascading joy beyond compare.
With each glance, a story told,
In the warmth, we break the cold.

Within quietude, we thrive,
Underneath this hive, alive.
Together we shall lift the veil,
And let festivity prevail.

Embrace of the Eventide

Stretching hands toward twilight's grace,
As the stars begin to trace.
In the softening of light,
We gather close to share our night.

Whispers float on gentle breeze,
Laughter mingles with the trees.
As the sun sinks ever low,
Illuminated hearts will glow.

Music swirls, a lively beat,
In this pulse, we find our seat.
Every smile a beacon shines,
Drawing warmth across the lines.

Together, let us start to weave,
Threads of joy that we believe.
In this evening, love's estate,
Embraced by light, we celebrate.

Stillness Between the Stars

In the night sky, lanterns glow,
Whispers of joy in a gentle flow.
Children laugh, their wishes take flight,
Sparkling dreams in the depths of night.

Laughter dances on the cool breeze,
As pine trees sway with playful ease.
Bells ring softly from afar,
Echoing warmth beneath each star.

Candles flicker, shadows play,
On this bright and wondrous day.
Family gathers, hearts unite,
In the stillness, pure delight.

With every hug, and every song,
The spirit of love grows ever strong.
In this moment, all feels right,
Together we shine, a dazzling light.

Long Shadows

Under twilight's tender embrace,
Shadows lengthen in a dance of grace.
The streets are alive with vibrant hues,
As laughter mingles with evening blues.

Candles flicker in window panes,
This town alive with joyful gains.
Festive spirits fill the air,
With memories crafted and moments to share.

Children's laughter in the dark,
Sparking joy like a tiny spark.
Neighbors greet with warm delight,
Tonight the world feels just so bright.

From rooftops high, the echoes play,
In long shadows, we light the way.
Underneath this starlit dome,
We find together we're truly home.

Quiet Hearts

In the stillness, hearts align,
Gathered close, your hand in mine.
Whispers of dreams drift in the cold,
A tapestry of stories waiting to unfold.

Softly glowing, lanterns gleam,
Flickering light, like a gentle dream.
The warmth of voices, a cherished sound,
In quiet moments, solace is found.

Around the fire, tales are spun,
Of laughter, of loss, but mostly of fun.
With each shared glance, our bonds renew,
In festive stillness, love rings true.

As the night sky blankets our heads,
We find joy in the words unsaid.
Quiet hearts beat in perfect time,
Together, we dance, lost in rhyme.

Echoing through the Frozen Breath

In the frosty air, laughter rings,
A chorus of joy, the season brings.
Snowflakes twirl in the shimmering light,
Each one a wish, a soft delight.

Footprints trace paths on hallowed ground,
In playful silence, magic is found.
The chill of winter, embraced with glee,
Echoing laughter, wild and free.

As hot cocoa warms our hands,
We gather close, in joyous bands.
Stories shared by the fire's glow,
This festive cheer, we long to sow.

In every heart, a spark ignites,
Dreams take flight on winter nights.
Through frozen breath, our spirits soar,
In this celebration, we ask for more.

Beyond the Veil of Dusk

The horizon blazes with golden hue,
Dusk unfolds secrets, both old and new.
Festivities bloom as daylight departs,
In every whisper, a story starts.

Lanterns alight in a dazzling array,
Guiding our spirits through twilight play.
Singing together, our voices rise,
Beneath the canvas of starlit skies.

Colors of laughter paint the air,
Each moment cherished, beyond compare.
With friends and family, love we embrace,
In this festive night, we find our place.

As the moon casts its silver glow,
We dance and twirl, letting joy flow.
Beyond the veil where dreams are spun,
United we stand, forever one.

Serenity Unveiled

In the garden, lights twinkle bright,
Laughter dances, hearts take flight.
Joyful songs fill the fresh night air,
Together we celebrate, without a care.

Candles flicker, shadows play,
Moments cherished, here to stay.
With every smile, spirits rise,
In this realm, true happiness lies.

Friends gather 'round, stories unfold,
Warm hugs shared, memories gold.
In the glow of love's embrace,
Serenity thrives, a sacred space.

As the stars weave their gentle tune,
We dance beneath the watchful moon.
With every beat, our souls ignite,
Serenity unveiled in the soft twilight.

The Dream of Quiet Time

Whispers of peace in the gentle breeze,
Time slows down, inviting ease.
A cup of warmth in hands that glow,
Savoring moments, taking it slow.

Shadows stretch as the sun dips low,
Nature's canvas starts to show.
Leaves rustle softly as daytime fades,
In nuptials of silence, kindness pervades.

Candles are lit, flickering bright,
Illuminating dreams in the night.
Mirthful laughter fills the air,
In the dream of quiet time, we share.

With twilight's brush, the world feels new,
In this sacred space, we find what's true.
Together we dream, embracing the night,
In harmony's glow, everything feels right.

Inhale the Frigid Air

Snowflakes swirl, a sparkling dance,
Inhale the frigid air, take a chance.
Laughter erupts in the winter's glow,
As families gather, spirits flow.

Fireside chats, warm hands held tight,
Starlit wishes in the cold, clear night.
Joy explodes like a brilliant flare,
In moments shared, love fills the air.

With cocoa sipped from mugs of cheer,
Voices ring out, so sweet and clear.
Embrace the chill, let your heart soar,
Inhale the frigid air, crave more.

Bundled blankets, stories unfold,
In this winter wonder, we brave the cold.
Together we thrive, dreams in our sight,
Inhale the frigid air, pure delight!

Night's Cloak of Mystery

Under the stars, secrets arise,
Night's cloak wraps us in whispered lies.
Shadows flutter as dreams ignite,
Magic awakens in the still of night.

A symphony hums in the depths so deep,
Stories of old drift in dreams we keep.
Each twinkling star, a beacon of hope,
Guiding the wanderers, teaching to cope.

The moon bathes the world in silver light,
Adventures await in the heart of the night.
With laughter shared under the darkened sky,
In night's cloak of mystery, spirits fly.

As the dawn nears, the magic will fade,
Yet memories linger, softly arrayed.
Hold tight the night, let wonder abound,
In the cloak of mystery, joy is found.

A Tapestry of Night Whispers

Stars twinkle in delight,
While laughter fills the air,
Voices dance in the night,
With stories we all share.

The moon gleams like a crown,
As dreams begin to weave,
A tapestry renowned,
In which hearts believe.

Colors swirl and collide,
Painting joy on every face,
With warmth we gather side by side,
In this festive embrace.

Together we ignite flames,
Weaving wishes on the breeze,
In whispers, love reclaims,
This joyous night with ease.

Beneath the Incandescent Calm

Candles flicker softly bright,
As shadows play on walls,
Chiming bells in gentle night,
In harmony, joy calls.

Beneath the stars, we sway,
With a warmth that never ends,
Laughter echoes, come what may,
In this moment with friends.

The air is rich with cheer,
As colors burst and bloom,
With every heart sincere,
We chase away the gloom.

Each smile a golden thread,
In this bright, festive seam,
A tapestry we tread,
Creating memories that gleam.

Watchful Silence of Falling Snow

Snowflakes whispering down,
A soft blanket of white,
Nature wears a crystal gown,
In the calm of the night.

Children laugh, full of glee,
Making snowmen so round,
In this magical spree,
Where warmth and joy abound.

The world seems to stand still,
As pure frost hugs the ground,
Every heart feels the thrill,
In silence, joy is found.

Together we find delight,
In the soft glowing light,
With every flake that falls,
We celebrate the night.

Carved in Glistening Silence

Icicles hang like jewels,
In the stillness of the night,
Lighting up like precious tools,
With a twinkle, pure and bright.

The world is etched in grace,
As snow dances from above,
Carved in nature's warm embrace,
A canvas made with love.

With each breath, magic glows,
As flames flicker in the hearth,
In the air, a sweet repose,
Filling hearts with mirth.

Together, voices blend,
In the hush of falling snow,
A festival that won't end,
In every smile, we sow.

Glistening Quietude

The stars above begin to twink,
As laughter echoes through the streets,
Soft lights adorn the branches bare,
And joy and wonder gently meet.

With every step, a spark of cheer,
The winter's chill can't dim our glow,
Families gather, hearts so near,
While melodies of joy will flow.

A table set, a feast awaits,
In every dish, a story shared,
The warmth of love, it resonates,
In every heart, the spirit bared.

As snowflakes twirl, a dance begins,
With every twinkling, dreams take flight,
In glistening quietude we find,
A festive grace within the night.

Shadows Dance in the Still Night

The moonlight weaves through branches bare,
While shadows dance, a silent play,
Beneath the stars, we breathe the air,
Of winter's night, a grand ballet.

With laughter ringing, spirits high,
Around the fire, stories told,
A tapestry of joy and sigh,
In every glance, the warmth unfolds.

The chilly breeze, a gentle kiss,
As flickering flames paint golden dreams,
Wrapped in the warmth of friendship's bliss,
Each moment dances, or so it seems.

In whispered secrets, peace does dwell,
As festive hearts share tender sights,
And in that hush, we weave our spell,
When shadows dance in the still night.

The Lament of the Shortest Day

As daylight wanes, and shadows grow,
The world drapes on a silken sigh,
Yet in the twilight, soft hopes glow,
A promise whispered, never die.

Gather 'round, and raise a toast,
To laughter shared beneath the stars,
For even in the dark, we boast,
Of dreams that shine; they leave their scars.

With candles lit, we chase the night,
In cozy corners, warmth and grace,
Though daylight fades from our clear sight,
Festive spirits find their place.

So let us cherish every smile,
The fleeting moments come to play,
As we remember for a while,
The lament of the shortest day.

Time Stands Still

In every twinkle, time does pause,
The world adorned in festive hue,
With laughter ringing, breaking laws,
Of moments lost, we start anew.

A symphony of hearts in sync,
As joy ignites the chilly air,
We raise our glasses, hearts in link,
In this embrace, we lose our care.

As fireworks burst in colors bright,
Each spark a wish of hope and cheer,
The magic of this wondrous night,
Keeps time at bay, brings loved ones near.

So let the music play, take flight,
In every note, our spirits fill,
Together we shall dance till light,
And in this space, time stands still.

Stillness at Dawn's Edge

In the quiet glow of morning,
Soft whispers dance on the breeze,
Colors bloom in sweet harmony,
Nature stirs with gentle ease.

Birds sing songs of bright promise,
As sunbeams touch the dew-kissed ground,
Life awakens in vibrant notes,
A symphony of joy unbound.

Laughter weaves through open fields,
Children chase dreams in the sun,
Each moment glows with pure delight,
In stillness, the day has begun.

Together, we bask in the warmth,
As shadows stretch and play their game,
At dawn's edge, we gather in peace,
In this festive world, we'll remain.

Emptiness of the Frosted Earth

Whispers float in the icy air,
Nature dons a blanket so white,
The world sleeps under stars' soft gaze,
In silence, the heart feels delight.

Frosted patterns paint the windows,
Each crystal sparkles in the light,
Children build dreams of winter's charm,
Laughter echoes through the night.

While fires crackle and stories weave,
Warmth surrounds the festive cheer,
Together we gather and share,
Creating memories that endear.

In the emptiness, joy is found,
As lanterns glow against the dark,
Frosted earth, a canvas bright,
Illuminated by winter's spark.

Chants of the Darkened Sky

Beneath the vault of midnight blue,
Stars twinkle like hearts beating fast,
Voices rise in a soulful chorus,
Chants of joy from the present past.

Lively spirits twirl and leap,
As shadows dance under the moon,
Together, we celebrate life,
In this moment, we feel attune.

The chill of night wraps us in peace,
Bonfire's warmth ignites our souls,
Each laugh and song sends out a spark,
In unity, our spirit rolls.

As the darkened sky listens close,
We share our dreams with cosmic flight,
The festive air wraps around us,
In the night, we find our light.

Beneath the Weight of Starlight

Underneath the sprawling night,
Where starlight drapes like velvet sheets,
We gather close with hearts so bright,
In revelry, our joy repeats.

Fireflies flicker, dreaming small,
As tales are spun of olden days,
Together our laughter fills the air,
Echoing time in joyful ways.

With every toast to friendship's bond,
We celebrate what is to be,
In the warmth of love's embrace,
The world's a grand tapestry.

Beneath starlight, our spirits soar,
In the magic of moonlit glow,
Festive moments, we cherish deep,
In our hearts, the love will flow.

Gentle Tides of the Cosmic Sea

Waves of stars in a velvet night,
Sparkling laughter, a dazzling sight.
Whispers of comets dance and glide,
In the vastness where dreams reside.

Galaxies spin in a joyful swirl,
Celestial rhythms begin to twirl.
Colors of joy paint the endless skies,
A celebration where wonder lies.

Planets twinkle with blissful cheer,
Echoes of harmony fill the sphere.
As the universe sings its sweet tune,
We gather beneath the watching moon.

Cosmic tides bring us together near,
With a heart full of hope, we persevere.
In this festival of light and grace,
We find our joy in this lovely space.

Breath of the Frozen Universe

Icicles glisten in the morning sun,
A crystalline world where magic has spun.
Winter's embrace wraps us in its chill,
Yet warmth ignites, a glow we can feel.

Snowflakes dance like the softest cheer,
Each sparkling drop whispers, 'Hold dear.'
Merry hearts gather, laughter takes flight,
In the cold air, our spirits ignite.

Fires crackle, the embers glow bright,
Around the hearth, we share our delight.
A festive feast beneath twinkling stars,
Layered dreams wrapped in silver bars.

Celebrate moments, let worries cease,
In the frozen magic, we find our peace.
With every breath, a world so divine,
Together we weave our stories in time.

Silent Stories Told by the Moon

Under the gaze of a hushed silver light,
The moon whispers secrets throughout the night.
Gentle beams kiss the earth with embrace,
Unfolding tales in a tranquil space.

Stars twinkle softly, bear witness in awe,
To stories of lovers and dreams that we draw.
In every shadow, a memory gleams,
Echoes of wishes and woven dreams.

Time dances lightly on soft silver beams,
Writing our fables and ancient themes.
As the moon's glow lights our hearts from within,
We gather to listen, where tales begin.

In stillness, we find the magic of night,
As secrets unfold in the pale moonlight.
With every heartbeat, a vibrant refrain,
A festivity born in the stories of rain.

A Stillness Created

In the quiet hush of a twilight glow,
Peace settles softly, gentle and slow.
Whispers of nature, a serene embrace,
Inviting our souls to a tranquil space.

Moments of stillness, a breath to unwind,
Past chaos fades, and clarity shines.
In the calm heart of a shimmering lake,
Reflecting the joy that our spirits awake.

As fireflies twinkle, we gather in grace,
With laughter and warmth, we fill the space.
Under the stars, we share our delight,
In this tranquil moment, everything feels right.

So let us celebrate, with hearts intertwined,
In the magic of stillness, a world redefined.
With every heartbeat, life gently flows,
Creating a festivity that endlessly grows.

The Quietance of Endless Time

Beneath the stars, we dance tonight,
With laughter ringing, hearts feel light.
Moments pass like whispers, sweet,
In this stillness, our souls meet.

Candles glow in amber hue,
Reflections of the joy we brew.
Friendship woven, strong and true,
In this embrace, the world feels new.

Each tick of time a gentle sigh,
Echoing dreams that float up high.
We spin around in rosy bliss,
A tapestry of joy, we kiss.

Let every second swathe us whole,
In this quiet, we find our soul.
The endless hours weave a rhyme,
As we bask in the quietance of time.

A Breath Between Seasons

As autumn leaves begin to fall,
We gather near, we heed the call.
Hot cocoa warms our chilly hands,
A festive cheer, as laughter stands.

With winter's breath, the air turns crisp,
And every hug feels like a wisp.
We'll share our dreams by flickering flame,
In this space, we feel no shame.

Revelry dances on the breeze,
While snowflakes whisper through the trees.
In twilight's grasp, the world stands still,
Affected by seasons' sweet thrill.

In this breath, we pause, reflect,
On bonds that time cannot deflect.
A joyful heart sings loud and free,
In perfect harmony, you and me.

Enchanted by the Dark

The velvet night wraps us in peace,
An enchanted world, where worries cease.
Stars above twinkle in delight,
As shadows play, igniting the night.

Whispers of magic linger in air,
With moonlight's glow that we all share.
Bonfires blaze, creating dreams,
As gentle laughter flows like streams.

Moments weave like silver thread,
In darkness, we find paths to tread.
Every smile a spark, igniting cheer,
In this haven, the night feels near.

Wrapped in warmth of friendship strong,
We sway together, a blissful song.
Enchanted by the dark so deep,
Together, in this magic, we leap.

Flicker of Forgotten Flames

Amongst the embers, memories glow,
Flickering flames that dance so slow.
We reminisce, our voices blend,
In the warmth of the past, we transcend.

Time-worn stories fill the air,
With laughter rich, it's beyond compare.
Old friends gather, hearts entwined,
In every glance, love defined.

The fire crackles, whispers of old,
A tapestry of warmth retold.
We lift our cups to nights gone by,
In this fleeting moment, we fly.

Let these flames ignite anew,
In every heart, a spark breaks through.
As long as we gather, celebrate,
These flickers remind us: it's never too late.

Whispers of the Longest Night

In the hush of twilight glow,
Laughter dances, hearts aglow,
Twinkling lights on every tree,
Joyful whispers, wild and free.

Families gather, stories shared,
Warmth of love, no one spared,
Sipping cocoa, tales unfold,
Magic woven, bright and bold.

Outside, snowflakes whirl and play,
Every moment pure ballet,
Underneath the starlit sky,
We embrace the night, oh my!

Sparkling dreams in every heart,
From this night, we shan't part,
With each smile, the stars align,
Together, our spirits shine.

Echoes of Distant Stars

Glimmers twinkle in the night,
Echoes of fading daylight,
Gathered 'round the fire's cheer,
Whispers carried, love sincere.

Songs of joy fill every air,
Moments treasured, none to spare,
Hands entwined as shadows dance,
In this space, we find romance.

Underneath the vast expanse,
Hearts ignite in the moon's glance,
Every laugh, a star reborn,
A festive tapestry, well-worn.

Magic swirls with every cheer,
New beginnings draw us near,
In this glow, we find our way,
Echoes linger, night to day.

Twilight's Quiet Embrace

The twilight whispers gentle peace,
Colors blend, all worries cease,
In the garden, laughter blooms,
Joyful chatter fills the rooms.

Candles lit, their soft, warm glow,
Echoes of love in every flow,
Amidst the cheer, we raise our glass,
To moments fleeting, none shall pass.

Underneath the evening stars,
We share our dreams, near and far,
Every heartbeat, sweet as wine,
In each glance, the world's divine.

Together we weave the night,
Every moment feels so right,
In twilight's arms, we find our place,
Lost in joy, forever grace.

Shadows Beneath the Winter Moon

In the winter's crisp embrace,
Moonlight bathes this sacred space,
Shadows dance upon the ground,
In their waltz, pure joy is found.

Snowflakes glisten in the light,
Candles flicker, spirits bright,
Neighbors gather, laughter springs,
Songs of joy as sweet bells ring.

With every cheer, the night's aglow,
Stories shared in fragments slow,
Underneath this starry quilt,
Bonds of love and hope are built.

As we gather, hearts entwine,
Moments treasured, pure and fine,
Shadows play beneath the moon,
Together, we will sing our tune.

Interlude of Glimmering Stars

In twilight's embrace, we gather near,
Laughter and joy, a festive cheer.
Candles flicker, their flames dance bright,
Hearts are warmed in the soft twilight.

Songs drift gently on the cool breeze,
Whispers of hope among the trees.
With every toast, our spirits soar,
Magic unfolds, we yearn for more.

The stars above, like diamonds rare,
Radiate love, they fill the air.
Beneath this sky, we share our dreams,
Life's a canvas, or so it seems.

Together we'll revel, hand in hand,
Creating memories, perfectly grand.
Each moment cherished, a jewel to hold,
In this interlude, our hearts are bold.

Whispers of the Longest Night

Amidst the glow of lanterns bright,
We gather close on this longest night.
Joy spills forth like a flowing stream,
In laughter and love, we dance and dream.

The chill of winter cannot deter,
As warmth ignites in the hearts that stir.
Voices unite, a harmonious song,
In the embrace of friends, we belong.

Snowflakes fall like soft confetti,
Each flake a shimmer, the world is ready.
As sparks fly high from the crackling fire,
Our spirits soar, we rise ever higher.

Whispers of love under the starlit dome,
In these precious moments, we find our home.
Wrapped in the magic of this special night,
Together we shine, our futures bright.

Echoes in the Stillness

In the hush of night, the world takes pause,
Echoes of laughter, a gentle cause.
Candles illuminate the paths we walk,
In silent communion, hearts gently talk.

The sweetness of dreams hangs in the air,
As friends and family gather to share.
With every toast, memories unfold,
Stories retold, both new and old.

The stillness hums with the joy of now,
Moments we cherish, we take a bow.
Under the moon's soft, silvery glow,
We weave our tales in a rhythmic flow.

In the echoes, we find our song,
A tapestry woven, vibrant and strong.
With every heart beat, let the joy resound,
In this stillness, our love is profound.

Beneath the Shimmering Shadows

Beneath the trees where the shadows play,
Festive whispers carry the day.
Lights entwined in a lover's embrace,
We gather here, in this sacred space.

The air is sweet, like a sugary dream,
Laughter spills over, a joyful stream.
With every hug, our worries take flight,
In the magic of moments, hearts feel light.

Songs echo softly in the cool night air,
We sway together, without a care.
The stars peek through, a glittering veil,
In this tapestry, we shall not fail.

Beneath the shimmer, shadows take form,
In the pulse of the night, we find our warm.
As we raise a glass to the time we share,
In this festive glow, life is truly fair.

Solitary Glow

In the corner of a bustling street,
A lantern spills its warm light,
Flickering whispers of old days,
Glimmering dreams take flight.

Voices drift in the crisp night air,
Joyful laughter fills the scene,
Beneath the stars, hearts unite,
In a festive canvas, warm and keen.

Snowflakes dance like tiny sparks,
Collecting where moments align,
Each twinkle brings a memory,
In the glow, everything feels divine.

To celebrate the silent night,
With every light, a story's told,
In the stillness, we find delight,
In this glow, we all feel bold.

Lullabies of the Frozen Earth

Beneath the quilt of soft white snow,
Nature sings a gentle tune,
Crystals shimmer in the moonlight,
While dreams are wrapped in solitude.

Pines wear coats of frosty lace,
Children giggle and race about,
As echoes of joy fill the space,
In winter's wonder, there's no doubt.

Lanterns line the peaceful paths,
Each step a moment to embrace,
With hearts aglow in soft, warm baths,
The world rejoices, a perfect place.

In the silence, a sweet refrain,
Lullabies touch the sleeping earth,
Carols wrapped in winter's pain,
But within lies endless mirth.

Secrets in the Frost

As dawn breaks with a silver hue,
Frosty patterns tell their tale,
Whispered secrets of night's embrace,
Fragile beauty that won't pale.

Every breath, a clouded sigh,
Footsteps crunch on freshly laid,
Underneath the chilly sky,
Happiness and warmth cascade.

Winter's touch enchants the eye,
Painting fields in glistening white,
Every secret wrapped in sighs,
Festive spirits take to flight.

With mugs of cheer held high above,
We gather close to share the glow,
In frost's embrace, we find our love,
A dance beneath the shimmering snow.

Crystalline Hush

Amidst the silence, joy appears,
Crystalline whispers brush the air,
With every laugh, we shed our fears,
Threads of wonder everywhere.

At the window, frost paints scenes,
Glimmers of joy, so pure and bright,
In the stillness, there's something keen,
Harmonies dance in the night.

Hands are warmed by steaming cups,
As we share our tales of old,
With every smile, the spirit erupts,
In this moment, hearts unfold.

Beneath the stars, we stand as one,
Crystalline hush envelops all,
Under the moon, our thoughts are spun,
In the glow, we rise, we fall.

Dance of the Dimming Light

As twilight paints the skies aglow,
Whispers of magic begin to flow.
Footsteps of laughter fill the street,
In this moment, hearts skip a beat.

Balloons rise high, colors cascade,
Children's smiles never will fade.
The music plays, a sweet refrain,
Uniting souls, washing in the rain.

Candles flicker, shadows sway,
Hope sparkles as night meets day.
In every twirl, joy comes alive,
A festive spirit begins to thrive.

In unison, we lift our cheer,
Embracing love that draws us near.
With arms wide open, we celebrate,
This dance of life, oh it's so great!

Serenity of the Starlit Void

Under the canvas of the night,
Starry gems twinkle, pure delight.
Candles glow on every face,
In this hush, we find our place.

Whispers carried on the breeze,
Echoing softly through the trees.
A toast to dreams that gently soar,
A moment's peace, forevermore.

With every glance, we paint the sky,
In unity, our spirits fly.
The world can fade, but we remain,
In the starlit void, free from pain.

Here in the stillness, hearts align,
Together we taste the sweetest wine.
Serenity wraps us, truly blessed,
In this festive night, we find our rest.

Night's Velvet Embrace

A velvet sky holds the day's end,
Fireworks burst, and hopes transcend.
The joy spreads wide like a warm hug,
In every heartbeat, life's a snug bug.

Glistening lights dance on the lake,
Echoing laughter, a promise to make.
Children twirl in a carefree spin,
In this night, let the magic begin.

Cakes and sweets adorn every table,
Stories unfold, as long as we're able.
Hands raised high in a joyous cheer,
In night's embrace, we hold what's dear.

With every toast and every song,
Together in this, we all belong.
Under the stars, let our spirits roam,
In this festive realm, we find our home.

Muted Revelations

In shadows cast by flickering flames,
Secret truths call out our names.
The night is rich with whispered lore,
As laughter breaks, we seek for more.

Beneath the glow of lanterns bright,
We share our dreams beneath the night.
Each story told, a treasure found,
In muted tones, love spreads around.

The festive spirit swells the air,
Binding us with an unseen care.
In gentle smiles, we pass the dawn,
As new revelations carry on.

So let the night wrap us in grace,
In every heart, there's a special place.
Together we flourish, spirits unite,
In muted moments, purest light.

Hushed Moments in Winter's Grasp

Snowflakes twirl, a dance of white,
Whispers of joy in soft moonlight.
Fires crackle, warmth is near,
Hearts unite, spreading cheer.

Laughter bounces off the trees,
A chilly breeze brings memories.
Hot cocoa warms our tender hands,
In this wonder, love expands.

Footprints trace the path we've made,
Underneath the glistening shade.
Stars peek out from skies so deep,
In this moment, dreams we keep.

Together in this frosty night,
Wrapped in warmth, our souls take flight.
Every hush sings of delight,
In winter's grasp, we shine so bright.

A Lullaby for the Frozen Globe

Gentle snow, a tender sigh,
Underneath the starry sky.
Crystals dance on frozen streams,
Whispers weave through winter dreams.

Lullabies hum on the breeze,
Softly swaying, bending trees.
Blankets wrap the earth in peace,
In this stillness, worries cease.

Candles flicker, shadows play,
Lighting up the festive way.
Voices mingle, laughter sings,
Joy is found in simple things.

Night unfolds, the world's aglow,
In this magic, love will grow.
A lullaby, soft and sweet,
Embracing all who dare to meet.

When Time Pauses

Moments still, the clock stands slow,
In this pause, the joy will flow.
A gathering by the fireside,
With each smile, hearts open wide.

Twinkling lights adorn the night,
Everything glows, pure delight.
Faint melodies fill the air,
Secrets shared without a care.

Beneath the stars, we make a wish,
Wrapped in warmth, the world we relish.
As time stands still, we feel the thrill,
In this magic, our hearts are filled.

Every laugh, a melody bright,
Dancing shadows in the light.
When time pauses, we unite,
Creating moments, pure and right.

Secrets of the Silent Night

Amidst the hush, a secret shared,
In quiet corners, hearts are bared.
Whispers float on frosty air,
In winter's arms, we feel the care.

Glistening snow, a blanket snug,
Nights like this, we fall in love.
Softly spoken dreams take flight,
In the beauty of the night.

Twilight glows, a magical hue,
Under stars that shimmer true.
With every breath, a spark ignites,
Secrets bloom in tranquil nights.

Joyful memories we ignite,
In the warmth of silent nights.
With every cuddle, every cheer,
We hold the magic, forever near.

When Silence Speaks

In the heart of night, whispers play,
Dancing lights twinkle in a joyous array.
Laughter rises, fills the air,
Moments cherished, free of care.

Voices blend like a soft refrain,
A tapestry woven with laughter and gain.
Under the stars, dreams take flight,
In this festive hour, hearts feel so light.

Gathered together, spirits unite,
Sipping on joy, feeling so right.
Bells ring softly, a melodious tone,
In silent spaces, we find our home.

As the clock strikes, memories cast,
Moments of wonder, forever to last.
In the hush, where smiles ignite,
When silence speaks, everything feels bright.

Frosted Paths of Solitude

Snowflakes swirl like dances in air,
Whispered chill hugs the earth with care.
Each step taken leaves behind a trace,
On this frosted path, a gentle space.

Nature glistens, a canvas of white,
Under moon's glow, everything feels right.
Quiet reflections in the world's embrace,
In solitude's calm, we find our place.

Footprints lead to stories untold,
In the silence, warmth unfolds.
Hearts beat softly, a rhythmic tune,
In wintry woods beneath the moon.

Though paths may wind, we venture on,
In the stillness, we feel so strong.
Among the trees, our spirits roam,
On frosted paths, we're never alone.

Interludes of Calm

As the day unfolds, moments align,
Sunset paints skies in hues so fine.
Leaves whisper secrets on the breeze,
In interludes of calm, hearts find ease.

Shadows stretch gently, embracing the light,
Time takes a pause, everything feels right.
A symphony played by crickets and stars,
In tranquil evenings, we heal our scars.

Sipping on dreams, we breathe in deep,
In the quiet, tender memories seep.
Serenity beckons, a soft, sweet call,
Finding our rhythm, when stillness befalls.

The world slows down; we cherish the hour,
In these still interludes, we find our power.
Gathering moments like blossoms in bloom,
In a gentle hush, we craft our own room.

Stillness Beyond the Horizon

As dawn approaches, colors unfold,
Whispers of promise, stories untold.
The horizon beckons, a vast, bright sea,
In stillness beyond, we long to be free.

Mountains stand guard, ancient and grand,
In silence, they cradle the dreams we have planned.
With each gentle wave, hope starts to rise,
In the calm of the moment, underneath the skies.

Golden sun kisses the day awake,
In soft solitude, our fears start to break.
With every heartbeat, we journey anew,
In stillness, we gather the strength to break through.

Beyond the horizon, our spirits will soar,
Embracing the stillness, longing for more.
Together we stand, with hearts open wide,
In the dance of the universe, we joyfully glide.

The Weight of Darkness

In twilight's embrace, laughter rings,
Bright lanterns dance on gentle strings.
Colors swirl in the evening air,
While fireflies weave moments rare.

The chill of night can't dim our cheer,
With every heartbeat, love draws near.
Voices rise, a jubilant sound,
In this joy, our souls are found.

Underneath the stars' bright gaze,
We celebrate through the smoky haze.
Together we share a sacred space,
As the night wraps us in its grace.

So let the darkness fall around,
In our hearts, warmth will abound.
For in this festive night's delight,
We glow brighter than the night.

In the Company of Stars

Beneath the vast and endless sky,
Where dreams and wishes freely fly,
We gather close with hearts aglow,
In playful rhythm, our laughter flows.

The stars above twinkle and shine,
A cosmic feast, both yours and mine.
With each bright burst, we share our tales,
Of adventures vast like distant sails.

A chorus of voices fills the night,
In joyful harmony, pure delight.
Each moment cherished, together we're free,
In the company of stars, just you and me.

So raise a glass to friendships dear,
To memories made throughout the year.
In this celestial display so bright,
We find our joy, our shared delight.

Stillness of the Ascending Dawn

As dawn unfolds with golden grace,
Whispers of hope we gently trace.
The world awakens, crisp and clear,
In this stillness, joy draws near.

Colors blush across the sky,
While soft melodies flutter and fly.
Each breath we take, a gift anew,
In the quiet, the heart breaks through.

Gathered together, we share a sigh,
As light pours forth, we soar on high.
With every moment, laughter blooms,
In this magic, love consumes.

In the glow of a sun that's born,
We celebrate the end of mourn.
For in the stillness of this dawn,
We find our place, where joy goes on.

Softness of a Winter's Gaze

Snowflakes fall like whispers light,
Blanketing the world in white.
With every flake, our worries cease,
As winter's touch brings silent peace.

We gather 'round with smiles aglow,
Sharing stories in the fire's flow.
The warmth of friendship fills the air,
In this moment, nothing compares.

Outside, the chill wraps us tight,
But inside glows a fiery light.
Laughter dances through the space,
Binding hearts with gentle grace.

So let the snow fall, thick and fast,
As we embrace this joy amassed.
In winter's gaze, soft and clear,
We find our bliss, our love sincere.

Whispers of Ancient Constellations

In the night sky, dreams take flight,
Stars dancing, oh what a sight!
Laughter echoes through the air,
Magic woven everywhere.

Candles flicker, shadows play,
Voices rise, as children sway.
Under blankets, stories unfold,
Festivities bright, memories gold.

Colors burst, a vibrant hue,
Gathered hearts, both old and new.
Whispers travel, secrets shared,
In this moment, none compared.

The night ends with soft goodbyes,
But the joy forever lies.
In every heart, the stars will gleam,
Whispers of an endless dream.

Still Waters Run Deep

By the lake where silence reigns,
Joyful hearts break all the chains.
Reflections shimmer, ripples meet,
Nature sings, a rhythmic beat.

Beneath the moon, lanterns glow,
Gathered friends, in gentle flow.
Laughter dances on the breeze,
Moments cherished, hearts at ease.

In the depths, the secrets swell,
Tales of love we dare to tell.
As the stars fade, dawn draws near,
Still waters hold what we hold dear.

Though the night may pass away,
Memories of joy will stay.
Every heartbeat sings so sweet,
In stillness, life feels complete.

The Calm Before the Rebirth

In the hush before the dawn,
Hope arises, dreams are drawn.
Flowers sleep, beneath the earth,
Anticipation, life's rebirth.

Whispers float on gentle air,
Promises of joy laid bare.
Nature stirs, a sacred dance,
Each moment holds a hidden chance.

Crimson rays will greet the day,
In their warmth, we find our way.
Gathered close, with hands entwined,
In the calm, our souls aligned.

Celebrate what's yet to come,
Beating hearts, a steady drum.
As the sunlight breaks the night,
We embrace the pure delight.

The Echo of Stars

Echoes travel across the night,
Stars above, with pure delight.
They twinkle softly, tales unfold,
In each shimmer, dreams retold.

Gathered shadows, voices blend,
Every story, time will lend.
Whispers linger, laughter flows,
In the starlit, magic glows.

Footsteps light on paths once paved,
In this moment, hearts are saved.
Underneath the glowing dome,
Each star a guide, we find our home.

As the night begins to wane,
Hope ignites in joy's refrain.
With every echo, love will shine,
In the dance of space and time.

Time Held in Suspense

Laughter dances through the air,
Colors sparkle everywhere,
A moment savored, pure delight,
In joyous glee, we hold the night.

Balloons float with dreams untold,
Underneath the moonlight's gold,
Whispers of a soft romance,
In this magic, we find our chance.

The clock ticks slow, yet hearts race fast,
Moments like this, we wish to last,
Together we'll create our lore,
As happiness opens every door.

Let the music rise and swell,
Each note a cherished, secret spell,
Time held close, like a sweet embrace,
In this festival, we find our place.

Secrets of the Lengthening Shadows

The sun dips low, the sky aflame,
Whispers of dusk call out our name,
Secrets weave through the twilight haze,
In every corner, mystery plays.

The shadows stretch and begin to dance,
Inviting laughter, a sweet romance,
Candles flicker, casting soft light,
In this moment, the world feels right.

Gather 'round as the stories unfold,
Each tale a treasure waiting to be told,
With our hearts open and spirits bright,
We embrace the secrets of the night.

This festive air is rich and warm,
With hugs and smiles, we break the norm,
In the shadows, friendship glows,
Creating memories as the evening flows.

Between the Hours of Light

Sunrise paints the sky aglow,
Soft laughter lingers, spirits flow,
In the space where day greets night,
A fleeting moment, pure delight.

Festive banners dance in the breeze,
Joyful hearts, as sweet as ease,
The clinking glasses, toasts aflame,
In this rhythm, we're all the same.

Games and stories fill the air,
With every smile, we shed our care,
In the hours that feel like gold,
Memories born, stories unfold.

As twilight draws its velvet curtain,
We celebrate the bonds that strengthen,
Between the light, we find our cheer,
In this moment, together near.

Embrace of the Waiting Night

A gathering glow as dusk descends,
With open arms, the evening lends,
Laughter twinkles under the stars,
As we dance between worlds, near and far.

The air is laced with songs of cheer,
In the embrace of friends so dear,
With every note, our souls ignite,
Igniting dreams in the waiting night.

Feasts laid out with colors bright,
Celebrating love, pure and right,
Moments that shimmer, a joyful sight,
In this embrace, we find our light.

As shadows stretch and stars take flight,
We hold each other, hearts so light,
In the hours that promise delight,
Together we shine, in the waiting night.

The Calm Before the Light

The sun dips low, a gentle sigh,
Whispers of joy as night draws nigh.
Beneath the glow of lanterns bright,
We gather close, hearts intertwined.

Laughter dances on the breeze,
As shadows stretch, the world at ease.
In this moment, spirits soar,
A festive calm, we all adore.

Stars Holding Their Breath

In velvet skies, the stars align,
Each twinkle holds a wish divine.
A hush enfolds the earth below,
As dreams take flight, soft and slow.

Gathered wishes, bright yet meek,
In the stillness, magic speaks.
With a sparkle and a cheer,
Stars hold dreams, the night draws near.

The Art of Stillness

In quiet corners, candles glow,
Soft reflections, warmth we know.
A tapestry of joy unfolds,
As hearts together, tales retold.

Silence wrapped in love's embrace,
A gentle smile upon each face.
In the stillness, life's sweet blend,
A festive spirit, moments mend.

Frostbitten Dreams

The winter air, a crisp delight,
With frosty breath, we greet the night.
Snowflakes swirl, a dance so free,
Creating worlds of mystery.

Children laugh, their cheeks aglow,
In search of treasures, joy in tow.
Frostbitten dreams, alive they gleam,
A festive wonder, a shared team.